ANNE FRANK

Previous page: Anne Frank's diary. Anne's father gave her this red-checked diary on her 13th birthday. She wrote in it nearly every day.
Opposite: This photograph of Anne was taken around 1940. She is about 11 years old and standing outside her home in Amsterdam.

ANNE FRANK

"NOBODY NEED WAIT A SINGLE MOMENT BEFORE STARTING TO IMPROVE THE WORLD"

ANN KRAMER

QED Publishing

CONTENTS

EARLY YEARS

AN ORDINARY LIFE

THE SECRET ANNEXE

3

DISCOVERY AND DEPORTATION

4

EARLY
YEARS

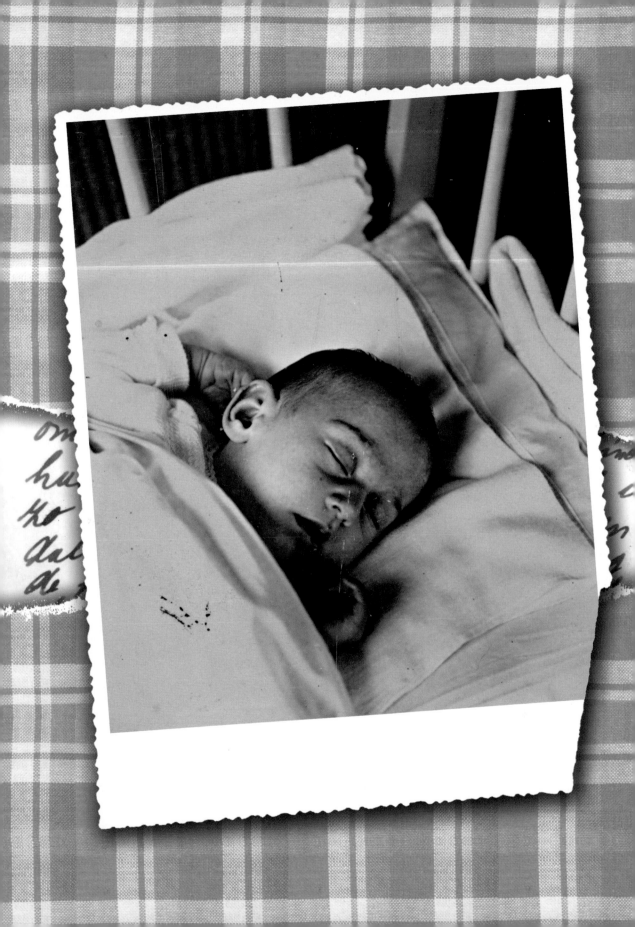

A Silver Necklace

Anne Frank was a young Jewish girl who lived during World War II (1939–45). She and her parents went into hiding to escape persecution, and she wrote a diary about the events. She died in a concentration camp, at the age of 15, but her diary survived and is world famous.

Anne was born in 1929 in Frankfurt, Germany. She came from a middle-class Jewish family. Her father was Otto Frank. He was a calm, thoughtful man, and Anne adored him her whole life. Her grandmother on her father's side was Alice Frank-Stern, whose ancestors had lived in Frankfurt for more than 400 years.

Otto was one of four children. He had two brothers, Robert and Herbert, and a younger sister known as Leni. According to Anne, her father had enjoyed 'a real little rich boy's upbringing'.

Previous page: Anne Frank sleeping in her cot. Her father, Otto, took this photograph soon after her birth.

Left: Edith Hollander and Otto Frank married in this synagogue in Aachen. Otto was 36 and Edith 25. It was a splendid wedding.

20 April 1889

Adolf Hitler, who later becomes dictator of Germany, is born in Austria.

12 May 1889

Otto Frank (Anne's father) is born in Frankfurt-am-Main, Germany.

Right: Margot Frank sits in a wicker chair on the balcony of her Frankfurt home, holding her baby sister, Anne. The photo was taken in 1929.

Jews' Lane

Anne's ancestors had lived in a ghetto in Frankfurt called the Judengasse (Jews' Lane). It was built in 1460 to keep Jews separate from Christians. The ghetto consisted of a curved lane with three gates, which were locked at night. By the 1500s, some 3,000 Jews lived in the Judengasse. It was pulled down in the late 19th century.

There were parties, banquets and a big house. Otto was well educated and had a passion for art and literature. He spent a short time in New York, working at Macy's department store, then returned to Germany to work in the family banking business.

During World War I (1914–18), Otto fought in the German army, reaching the rank of lieutenant. In 1924, he met Edith Hollander, a fashionable young Jewish woman. The Hollanders were wealthy manufacturers from Aachen. Edith loved art and music and, like Otto, was one of four children. Otto and Edith married in 1925, and their first daughter, Margot, was born a year later.

For a while the family lived with Otto's mother, sister and brother. In 1927, they moved into their own home, a spacious apartment at 307 Marbachweg in Frankfurt. Their second daughter was Annelies Marie (known as Anne). When Anne was born, she was given a silver necklace and pendant bearing the words 'Lucky Charm' and her date of birth.

16 January 1900

Edith Hollander (Anne's mother) is born in Aachen, Germany.

1914–18

World War I. Otto Frank serves in the German army. He has a reputation for bravery and is made a lieutenant.

Jews in Europe

There were more than 9 million Jews living in Europe when Anne was born. In some places, such as in Eastern Europe, Jews tended to live rather separate lives from non-Jews, following strict traditional Jewish laws and speaking their own language, Yiddish. Elsewhere, in Germany, France, Hungary and the Netherlands, Jews were assimilated, or mixed, into the population. Some were Orthodox, meaning they followed Jewish laws strictly, but many German Jews, such as Anne's family, were Liberal or Reform, and were not so rigid in following Jewish laws. They lived mainly in the cities. They went to synagogue, ate kosher food and observed Jewish religious festivals, such as Passover, Hanukkah and Yom Kippur, but also went to state-run schools and mixed with non-Jews.

Life for European Jews, however, had rarely been easy. They had experienced centuries of anti-Semitism (hatred of Jews). At different times, they had been moved from one town to another or forced to live in ghettos separately from Christians. From the mid-19th century, Jews in Germany had gained equal legal status with non-Jews.

But anti-Semitism was reappearing in the most brutal form ever known. In 1919, a new extreme political party was formed, known from 1920 as the National Socialist German Workers' Party (Nazi Party). Its leader was Adolf Hitler, a man who loathed the Jewish people. Under his direction, the Nazi Party began to persecute Jews.

Right: For Jews, the Torah is the most sacred document. It contains the Ten Commandments, which Jews believe were given directly to them by God. Torah means 'teaching'.

THE SYNAGOGUE

Jews attend synagogue to worship and study. Rabbis (teachers) lead religious services and hold classes for Jewish children. There were many synagogues in Germany, including the one pictured in Berlin (right). Some European Jews attended synagogue three times a week; others just once, on the Jewish Sabbath, which is Saturday.

Europe in 1933. Jews first arrived in Europe nearly 2,000 years ago. By 1933, Europe was home to some 9.5 million Jews. Three million Jews lived in Poland, and over 500,000 in Germany.

NORWAY
SWEDEN
ESTONIA
LATVIA
LITHUANIA
DENMARK
SOVIET UNION
POLAND
NETHERLANDS   Berlin
GREAT BRITAIN
GERMANY
Amsterdam
CZECHOSLOVAKIA
Aachen
Frankfurt
HUNGARY   ROMANIA
AUSTRIA
SWITZER-LAND
FRANCE
YUGOSLAVIA
BULGARIA
ITALY
ALBANIA
GREECE
SPAIN
PORTUGAL

Right: Passover is a major Jewish festival. It marks the time when, according to Jews, God 'passed over' the Israelites when he punished the ancient Egyptians. Jews throughout Europe celebrated Passover within the family, lighting candles and eating a special meal. The family plays a very important role in Jewish life.

An Inquisitive Child

The Franks' first home was a large rented apartment in a modern building. It had shuttered windows and a rear balcony, which Edith filled with potted plants. The apartment was full of books and Edith's antique furniture.

Even before she could walk, Anne was a lively, inquisitive child. Edith used to put her in a cot on the balcony, and she watched all the activities around her with great interest. The Franks were a close family. They visited Otto's mother regularly, and Anne's cousins – Buddy and Stephan, who were slightly older – were frequent visitors. On one occasion, Buddy and Stephan took Anne out in the pram. They raced around the street with the pram, which tipped up on the kerb, throwing Anne out. Fortunately, she was unharmed. Stephan often made Anne and Margot laugh, mimicking the silent film star Charlie Chaplin. At the weekends, they visited Edith's mother, Rosa, or took day-trips.

For Anne and Margot life was happy, but outside the home trouble was brewing. Germany was facing increasing economic problems and many people were poor.

Stormtroops

In 1921, Adolf Hitler created a special 'Storm Section' within the Nazi Party. Known as Stormtroops, or SA, they wore brown uniforms bearing the swastika, the Nazi symbol. During the late 1920s, they harassed and bullied Jewish people on the street.

1919
Adolf Hitler joins the German Workers' Party, later the Nazi Party. He becomes leader in 1921.

1923
Hitler tries unsuccessfully to seize power in Munich. He is sentenced to five years in prison.

'She [Anne] was a happy girl and a lively girl, and a playful girl. She was very intelligent and very bright.'

Buddy Elias, Anne's cousin, in an interview

The Nazi Party was gaining support. In 1927, the party had some 40,000 members. By 1933, the Nazi Party membership had grown to more than 2 million. Adolf Hitler made many speeches attacking the Jewish population, while Nazi propaganda helped whip up anti-Jewish feeling.

The Franks' landlord was a Nazi sympathizer who did not want Jews in his building. In March 1931, when Anne was nearly two, the Franks had to leave. Otto moved the family to a new apartment at 24 Ganghoferstrasse, in an area of Frankfurt known as the Poets' Quarter.

Above: Otto Frank with his two daughters, Margot on the left and Anne on the right. The sisters were very different. Margot was quiet and shy, while Anne was chatty and asked questions constantly.

12 May 1925
Otto Frank and Edith Hollander marry in Aachen, Germany.

18 July 1925
Hitler publishes *Mein Kampf* (*My Struggle*), in which he describes his wish to eliminate Jews from Europe.

Left: Anne stands in a sandpit with her mother nearby (Frankfurt, 1931). Otto was an avid photographer and took many photos of his daughters, recording every event of their young lives. Many of the photographs have survived and give a detailed picture of Anne's early life.

Made-up stories

Otto amused his daughters by telling them made-up stories. Anne particularly enjoyed stories he told them about two make-believe sisters – Good Paula and Bad Paula. Much later, Anne wrote her own stories about them.

The apartment was smaller, but there was a large garden where Anne and Margot played. The neighbourhood was full of children, and the sisters made many friends, playing together in noisy groups. When it snowed, they went tobogganing on nearby hills, with Margot pulling her little sister on a sled.

Despite the growing anti-Jewish feeling, the family continued to live as normal. Margot started school in 1932 and loved it. She also went to classes to learn about the Jewish religion. Edith had come from a leading Jewish family in Aachen and was quite religious. She went regularly to synagogue and followed Jewish dietary laws, using only kosher food.

16 February 1926

Margot Betti Frank is born in Frankfurt, Germany.

12 June 1929

Annelies Marie Frank (known as Anne) is born in Frankfurt, Germany.

Otto was more liberal: he encouraged Margot and Anne to learn about different religions and beliefs, not just Judaism. The two girls had friends of different religious faiths: Jewish, Catholic and Protestant. On one occasion, Margot attended a Catholic friend's Holy Communion ceremony.

Otto valued education. He encouraged his daughters to take up hobbies and interests and, as they grew older, suggested that they make full use of his growing collection of books. He wanted them to be broad-minded and informed. By this time, Otto's banking business was failing. Their apartment was too expensive, and in 1933, they moved in with Otto's mother once more.

Below: Anne had many relatives and friends. This photograph shows Anne when she was a little girl (standing, third from the left). Her sister Margot is fourth from the right, and her much-loved cousin Buddy is lying on the far left.

October 1929
The New York Stock Exchange crashes, causing worldwide economic depression by 1931.

1930–33
Germany is ruled by exceptional legislation, and democracy is steadily eroded.

Leaving Frankfurt

The Frank family tried to continue life as normal, but conditions in Germany were getting worse. Unemployment was widespread, and Hitler and the Nazis were growing in power.

Hitler blamed Jews and Communists for Germany's problems. Many Germans agreed. The idea of 'race' was central to the Nazis' thinking. They believed that their own 'race' of white northern Europeans was superior to all other 'races', such as the Jews. They defined the Jews as a race rather than as followers of a religion. In 1932, in national elections, the Nazi Party won 37 per cent of the vote, making them the largest political party in the Reichstag (German parliament). In Anne's hometown, Frankfurt, the Nazi Party won the local elections. They celebrated with an anti-Jewish demonstration.

Left: Nazi Stormtroopers march through Nuremberg in 1933.

January–March 1933
Adolf Hitler becomes Chancellor of Germany. The Gestapo – Secret State Police – is formed.

March–April 1933
In Germany, Jewish businesses are boycotted. Jews are banned from teaching and from government jobs.

Right: A Hitler Youth rally in the 1930s. The Hitler Youth was formed in 1926 for non-Jewish boys 10 to 18. It aimed to teach Nazi values. In 1928, a girls' organization was created.

Hitler was asked to form a government and in 1933 was made Chancellor (President). He soon became dictator by passing laws such as the Law for Protection of People and State and the Enabling Act, which took away German citizens' key civil liberties, such as freedom of expression and freedom of the press. Hitler also began introducing anti-Jewish laws. Jewish businesses were boycotted and Jewish children were forbidden to go to school with non-Jewish children.

Leaving Germany

In 1933, 63,000 German Jews left Germany, including some of Anne's relatives. Her uncles Herbert and Robert went to France and England. Her grandmother Alice, Leni and husband Erich, and cousins Buddy and Stephan moved to Basel, Switzerland, in 1931. After the war, surviving relatives provided memories about Anne's early life.

The Franks knew it was now too dangerous to stay in Germany, and Otto made plans to leave. Edith's brother had a business in Switzerland and suggested Otto start a branch in Amsterdam, in the Netherlands. The company distributed pectin, a thickening agent used to make jam. Anne, Margot and Edith went to Aachen to stay with Edith's mother while Otto went to Amsterdam to find a home. Edith and Margot joined him in December 1933. Anne arrived two months later.

May–July 1933
Books by Jewish and 'un-German' authors are burned publicly. Hitler bans all political parties except the Nazi Party.

September 1933
Otto Frank leaves Germany and sets up Opekta works in Amsterdam, the Netherlands.

AN ORDINARY
LIFE

A Fresh Start

Anne was four years old when she arrived in Amsterdam. After the dangers in Germany, Amsterdam offered safety and a new start.

Above: A label advertising Opekta, the company that Otto Frank ran. Otto designed the advertisements himself.

Previous page: A passport photograph taken in May 1938 (bottom), a month before Anne's ninth birthday, and a photo taken three years later, in May 1941.

The Franks rented a five-room apartment at 37 Merwedeplein in an area known as the River Quarter. Amsterdam is full of canals. One tree-lined canal ran near their home, and there was a river behind the apartment building. The Franks rented out one of their rooms and filled the apartment with furniture brought from Frankfurt, including Edith's favourite antiques: a writing desk and grandfather clock. Modern sculptures decorated the apartment.

Anne's neighbourhood was a bustling area, full of shops and coffeehouses. Other Jewish people also lived in the area. Many, like the Franks, were refugees who had fled from Germany. There were some tensions between the newcomers and Dutch Jews, but at that point it was, on the whole, easy for German Jews to enter the Netherlands. Later, restrictions were introduced.

February 1934
Anne joins her family in Amsterdam. She starts studying at a Montessori school.

12 June 1934
Anne celebrates her fifth birthday with a party in her new home.

Right: This photograph shows some of the Opekta staff outside the office. Miep Santrouschitz (far left) did accounts and answered customer queries. Victor Kugler (far right) managed the staff.

Life in Amsterdam was going well for the Franks. They all learned to speak Dutch; Anne picked it up easily, although her mother found it more difficult. Otto's business, Opekta, was flourishing, and he moved it into new premises at 400 Singel. This was a large building above a floating flower market. He employed a small workforce. Two of the staff were from Austria – Miep Santrouschitz (later Gies) and Victor Kugler, who managed the staff. They were not Jewish but became very close family friends.

As life improved for the Franks in Amsterdam, conditions worsened for Jews in Germany. New laws were introduced, stripping Jews of their citizenship and all rights. Rumours of Jews being taken to internment camps and brutalized began to spread.

A birthday present

Anne arrived in Amsterdam at about the time of Margot's eighth birthday. Anne later wrote in her diary that she had been 'plonked down on the table as a birthday present for Margot'.

30 June 1934

The Night of the Long Knives: leading Nazis who have disagreed with Hitler's policies are murdered.

1 August 1934

Hitler becomes Führer (leader) of Germany and the supreme military commander.

School Days

Otto and Edith sent Anne and Margot to schools near where they lived. The girls suffered from health problems, but they both enjoyed school in their different ways.

Margot studied hard. Her parents and teachers saw her as a gifted pupil and she talked of going on to college when she was older. Anne found schoolwork more troublesome. She was active, demanding and did not like sitting still. For this reason, her father chose a Montessori school, where children were allowed to talk in class, learning was activity based, and she would have individual attention.

At first, Anne found learning to read difficult, but she enjoyed her school enormously. She made a strong impact on teachers and others around her. Sometimes, she walked to school with one of her teachers. Later, he remembered that she would chatter away, telling him about stories and poems that she and her father had made up.

Edith wrote letters to friends and relatives in Germany, telling them about her two daughters. She wrote about how hard Margot was studying and mentioned that Anne was finding it harder to 'buckle down' to schoolwork.

> *'When we were still part of ordinary, everyday life,*
> *everything was just marvellous.'*
> **Anne Frank, 'Do You Remember?'**

15 September 1935
In Germany, the Nazi Party passes the Nuremberg Laws, which define Jews as non-German and racially inferior.

8 March 1936
German troops march into the Rhineland, a demilitarized zone between Germany and France.

Even so, both parents commented that their younger daughter was amusing and fun, even if she could be difficult at times.

Anne and Margot were not physically very strong. Anne was often ill. She had a weak heart and suffered from rheumatic fever. She was supposed to rest most afternoons and was not allowed to play sports at school. But she did gymnastics, which she enjoyed, and outside school, learned to swim and ice-skate, activities that she loved. During the summer, the sisters spent time in the fresh air, at a local beach, which helped to improve their health.

Below: This photograph, taken in 1935, shows Anne's school class. Anne is sitting at the back, in front of her teacher. An Italian, Dr Maria Montessori, founded Montessori schools. She believed children should learn at their own pace through fun activities.

Shocking the adults

Anne's arms and legs sometimes dislocated, or came out of their sockets. She loved to shock adults by deliberately cracking her shoulder in and out of its socket.

Summer 1936
The Olympic Games are held in Germany. Hitler uses them as a showcase for Nazi might.

Summer 1936
The van Pels family flees Germany and arrives in the Netherlands. They later meet the Franks and become friends.

Making Friends

Anne made lots of friends. At school, her two best friends were Hanneli Goslar, who was called Lies, and Sanne Ledermann. The three spent so much time together they were nicknamed 'Anne, Hanne and Sanne'.

Lies's and Sanne's families were also German Jews. They had arrived in Amsterdam at about the same time as the Franks. The Goslar and Frank families became close friends. Anne and Lies were almost inseparable. They giggled together, told each other secrets, swapped postcards of the British and Dutch royal families and even shared childhood illnesses. In

Above: Anne and friends sitting in a sandpit. Anne, about eight years old, is second from the left. Hanneli, known as Lies, is sitting on the far left, and Sanne is standing up on the far right.

1936, both of them had measles at the same time. They were not allowed to visit while they were sick, but they telephoned each other every day.

After school and at weekends, the girls, together with other friends, played hopscotch and rushed about doing handstands and cartwheels. They called for each other to come out and play by whistling through the letterbox. Anne could not whistle, so she sang instead. There was a craze for keeping poetry albums. Friends wrote poems in each other's albums and decorated them with pictures.

26 October 1936
The Italian Fascist leader Benito Mussolini and Hitler form an alliance known as the Rome-Berlin axis.

16 July 1937
Buchenwald concentration camp opens near the German town of Weimar.

Edith was sometimes homesick for friends and family in Germany. She wrote regular letters, and the family visited her mother in Aachen and Otto's family in Switzerland.

Both the Franks and Goslars observed the Jewish festivals, although the Goslars were more devout Jews than the Franks. The Franks usually spent Friday nights, the start of the Sabbath, at the Goslars' house, and they often celebrated Passover together. The Franks also celebrated Christmas, something the Goslars did not do. Edith went to synagogue regularly, but Anne preferred to spend Saturdays playing in Otto's office.

Going to synagogue

Edith was closely involved with a Liberal Jewish synagogue in Amsterdam. Lies studied Hebrew on Wednesdays and Saturdays. Margot also took Hebrew classes. She took religion more seriously than Anne and said she wanted to be a nurse in Palestine when she grew up.

Below: Anne, Margot and two other Jewish refugee girls enjoy a tea party and playing with their dolls. Between 1933 and 1938, about 25,000 German Jewish refugees arrived in Amsterdam.

13 March 1938
Germany annexes (takes over) Austria in Hitler's first move toward creating a 'Greater Germany'.

September 1938
The Munich Agreement: Britain allows Germany to take over the Sudetenland, an area of Czechoslovakia.

Kristallnacht

By 1938, life for Jews in Germany had become very dangerous. They had been stripped of their citizenship, taken out of the military and barred from a whole range of jobs and public places. Hitler was determined to rid Germany of all Jews. In 1938, some 17,000 Polish Jews, many of whom had lived in Germany for years, were forced out of Germany. The son of two of the deportees, Herschel Grynszpan, lived in Paris. He went to the German Embassy there and killed a Nazi official to protest his parents' deportation.

This gave the Nazis the excuse they needed to launch a brutal attack on German Jews. In November 1938, in what became known as Kristallnacht (the Night of Broken Glass), organizations such as the Schutzstaffel, or SS (Defence Squadron), destroyed 7,500 Jewish businesses, set fire to synagogues, burned sacred Jewish books and vandalized Jewish cemeteries. Jews were attacked and beaten: 91 died and 26,000 were arrested and sent to concentration camps. Some historians have said Kristallnacht marked the true start of the Holocaust.

Below: A synagogue burns during Kristallnacht. During the night of 9–10 November 1938, Nazis burned and looted nearly 200 synagogues, including the one in Aachen where Anne's parents had married.

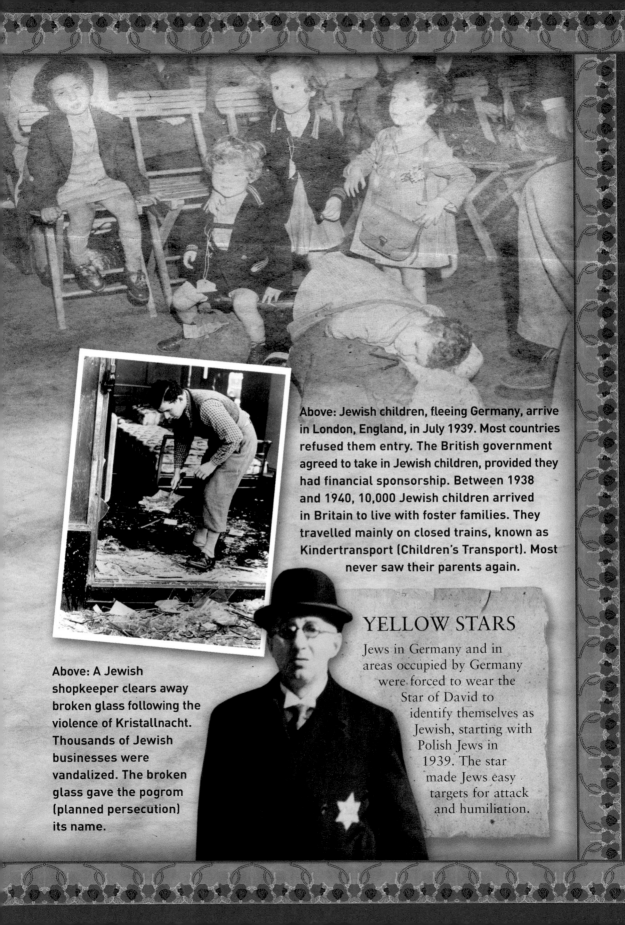

Above: Jewish children, fleeing Germany, arrive in London, England, in July 1939. Most countries refused them entry. The British government agreed to take in Jewish children, provided they had financial sponsorship. Between 1938 and 1940, 10,000 Jewish children arrived in Britain to live with foster families. They travelled mainly on closed trains, known as Kindertransport (Children's Transport). Most never saw their parents again.

Above: A Jewish shopkeeper clears away broken glass following the violence of Kristallnacht. Thousands of Jewish businesses were vandalized. The broken glass gave the pogrom (planned persecution) its name.

YELLOW STARS

Jews in Germany and in areas occupied by Germany were forced to wear the Star of David to identify themselves as Jewish, starting with Polish Jews in 1939. The star made Jews easy targets for attack and humiliation.

Growing Up

Anne's circle of Jewish and non-Jewish friends was growing. By the time she was about nine years old, she was developing an interest in fashion and boys. Lies and Anne were as friendly as ever, but Lies noticed that Anne enjoyed flirting, curling her hair around her fingers and glancing at boys.

Anne's schoolwork was improving. She hated maths but enjoyed history, drawing and essay-writing. According to one of her teachers, she was thinking of being a writer one day. Anne loved having fun and was always the centre of attention. She had very strong views and could be temperamental.

In 1938, Anne, Margot and Otto visited Otto's mother in Switzerland. Anne and her cousin Buddy spent time together, dressing up and pretending to be film stars. It was the last time they met. The same year, Otto opened a second business, Pectacon, which dealt in herbs and spices. He employed an old friend, Johannes Kleiman, as accountant for both firms.

Left: Anne lying on a beach with her sister, Margot, in 1940, when Anne was 11. The sisters often went to this resort, which was near Amsterdam.

9–10 November 1938
Kristallnacht (the Night of Broken Glass): Nazis kill 91 Jews and loot Jewish businesses.

12–15 November 1938
26,000 German Jews are arrested and sent to concentration camps.

> *'My mother, who liked Anne, would say, "God knows everything, but Anne knows everything better."'*
>
> Hanneli Goslar

Right: Anne loved the movies and dreamed of going to Hollywood. For her 13th birthday party, her father rented a film starring Rin Tin Tin, a German shepherd dog.

He also asked a fellow German Jew, Hermann van Pels, to be business adviser. Van Pels; his wife, Auguste; and their son, Peter, had arrived in Amsterdam from Germany in 1936. They lived nearby.

Every Saturday, the Franks welcomed guests to their home. These included the van Pels; Miep and her boyfriend Jan Gies, a Dutchman who worked in the social services; and Fritz Pfeffer, a Jewish dentist who had fled Germany after Kristallnacht. Discussion centred on events in Germany. Otto tried to remain optimistic that Hitler might be overthrown, but Edith was less so.

In June 1939, Anne celebrated her tenth birthday with a special party and picnic to mark moving into double figures. War was looming and there were fears of a German invasion. A relative in England wrote to Otto suggesting that he send Anne and Margot to live with them for safety. Otto refused because he and Edith could not bear to be parted from them.

March 1939
Anne's maternal grandmother, Rosa Hollander, leaves Germany to live with Anne and her family in Amsterdam.

15 March 1939
Germany takes over all of Czechoslovakia. Britain and France agree to support Poland if it is invaded.

War and Invasion

In September 1939, Germany invaded Poland. Britain and France declared war on Germany, and World War II began. In May 1940, Germany invaded the Netherlands.

Margot was 14 and Anne nearly 11 when German troops marched into the Netherlands. The girls were growing up fast. Anne loved cinema and drama, often writing plays and acting in them at school. She was an excellent mimic and made people laugh imitating her teachers, friends and even her cat, Moortje. Anne also fell briefly in love with a 14-year-old boy at her school.

Below: Nazi troops in armoured vehicles drive through Amsterdam. Germany invaded the Netherlands on 10 May 1940. The Dutch royal family fled to London.

The Germans promised everyone that life would continue as normal, but that did not happen.

1 September 1939
German forces invade Poland. Britain and France declare war on Germany on 3 September. World War II begins.

May 1940
Germany invades Denmark, Norway, the Netherlands, France, Belgium and Luxembourg.

Between 1940 and 1942, Jews in the
Netherlands, including the Franks,
were forced to register, carry identity
cards and wear the Star of David. They
were removed from work, forbidden to
go to certain cafes and restaurants, and
banned from parks, swimming pools and
ice-skating rinks. They were not allowed
to use public transportation. Anne later
wrote in her diary about how, because they
were Jews, their lives were restricted.

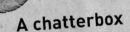

A chatterbox

Anne had a keen sense of humour.
She talked constantly in class. As
punishment, her teacher told her
to write an essay entitled 'A
Chatterbox'. Anne wrote three
pages arguing that talking was a
female trait and that she would
never break the habit because her
mother was so talkative.

In December 1940, Otto moved his business to new premises at 263
Prinsengracht. Jewish businesses now had to be registered. He changed the
company's name to Gies and Company, to prevent its falling into German
hands. In 1941, a new law forced Anne and Margot to leave their schools.
Anne was upset and cried when she said goodbye to her headmistress. She,
Margot and Lies went to a nearby Jewish school, where Anne soon made new
friends, including a girl called Jacqueline. They often met at Anne's home,
swapped pictures of film stars and played board games. Anne's home became a
mini-cinema. Otto rented films, and Anne made tickets and invited friends.
Edith handed out sandwiches, and Otto showed the films on a home projector.

'After May 1940 the good times were few and far between:
first there was the war ... then the arrival of the Germans, which is
when the trouble really started for the Jews.'
Anne Frank, diary, 20 June 1942

September 1940
Japan signs the Tripartite Pact
with Germany and Italy, making
them allies.

16 July 1941
Miep marries Jan Gies. Anne and her
father go to the wedding.

THE SECRET
ANNEXE

3

Into Hiding

By 1942, Nazis were rounding up Jews in the Netherlands for deportation to labour camps. Rumours grew that Jews were being worked to death or gassed. The Jewish Council in Amsterdam tried to prevent deportations, but without success.

Otto applied for permission from the British authorities to take his family to England but he did not get it. He began planning to take the family into hiding to avoid deportation. There was an annexe behind his office that could be used. His friends among the staff agreed to help: Miep Gies, Johannes Kleiman, Victor Kugler and the secretary, Bep Voskuijl. Miep's husband, Jan, and Bep's father also decided to help, even though this meant risking their lives. Secretly, they made preparations – cleaning the annexe, moving in furniture and food, and covering the windows with paper. The van Pels would share the annexe. At first, Otto and Edith did not tell Anne about the plan to go into hiding.

Left: Anne often used a fountain pen that her grandmother Rosa had given her to write in her diary. In her first entry, she wrote, 'I hope I will be able to confide everything to you.'

Previous page: This photograph shows the back of Otto's business at 263 Prinsengracht. Anne and her family hid in the building for two years.

7 December 1941

Japan bombs the US fleet at Pearl Harbor. The United States enters the war against Germany, Italy and Japan.

20 January 1942

At the Wannsee Conference in Germany, Nazi official Reinhard Heydrich obtains full support for the killing of all Jews.

Resistance

Jews and non-Jews resisted the Nazis. In Amsterdam, Ernst Cahn, a German Jew who owned an ice cream parlour, threw ammonia at SS men. He was tortured and shot. In February 1941, following a *razzia* (roundup of Jews), Dutch workers went on strike in protest. It ended when the Nazis threatened to kill 500 Jews in retaliation.

Below: Possibly the last photograph taken of Anne before she and her family went into hiding in 1942. She was 13. Those who met her spoke of her huge expressive eyes, love of life and vibrant personality.

In January 1942, Anne's maternal grandmother, Rosa, died of cancer. For Anne's 13th birthday in June, she had a small party. Her favourite gift was a diary, given to her by her father. Soon afterward, Otto told Anne about the plans.

On 5 July 1942, Margot received a notice telling her to report for deportation. Plans swung into action. The family packed quickly. Anne packed her diary, old letters and schoolbooks. Miep and Jan collected the bags. Early the next morning, the family left the apartment for the last time. It was too dangerous for Jews to be seen in public carrying suitcases, so Anne wore many layers of clothes. At 7:30 a.m., Anne said goodbye to her cat, then she walked through the rain to the hiding place.

April–May 1942

Combined Allied forces, British and US, begin mass bombing of German cities.

May–June 1942

Sobibor, Treblinka and Auschwitz-Birkenau death camps are opened in Greater Germany and occupied Poland.

Life in the Annexe

There were eight people in the annexe: Anne, Margot, their parents, the van Pels and Mr Pfeffer, the Jewish dentist, who joined them later. Other people thought that the Franks had gone to Switzerland. Even Anne's friend Lies did not know they were still in Amsterdam.

The annexe, which Anne called the 'Secret Annexe', was a number of rooms behind and above Otto's office. A staircase led to the first room, where Otto, Edith and Margot slept. It was also a communal space. Anne and Mr Pfeffer shared a room next to it. The van Pels lived in a room above, and their son, Peter, slept in a tiny, damp storage room. Furniture was basic: divan beds, bookshelves, a gas stove, tables, chairs and cupboards. The Franks left all their beautiful furniture and possessions behind. The windows were always covered.

   Not everybody who worked for Gies and Company knew about the annexe, so everyone had to be as quiet as possible during working hours. They got up early, and washed and had breakfast before the office staff arrived. After that, they tiptoed around, sewing, reading, studying or playing board games so no one could hear them. They prepared lunch when the office staff took their lunch break. Afterward, they rested or read. Anne usually wrote in her diary.

> *'I see the eight of us in the Annexe as if we were a patch of blue sky surrounded by menacing black clouds.'*
> **Anne Frank, diary, 8 November 1943**

12 June 1942	6 July 1942
Anne is given a diary for her 13th birthday.	Anne and her family go into hiding.

After the working day ended, people could relax and move around more freely, talking and preparing their evening meal. Sometimes Anne danced or did gymnastics. They went downstairs to the back office to listen to the radio for news of the war's progress.

No one could ever go outside or open or look out of the windows, in case someone saw them. Sometimes, at night, Anne peeked out of the attic windows or looked up at the sky. She loved to hear the church bells nearby. She hated being kept inside, and she missed her friends and her cat.

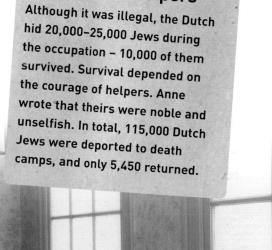

Courageous helpers

Although it was illegal, the Dutch hid 20,000–25,000 Jews during the occupation – 10,000 of them survived. Survival depended on the courage of helpers. Anne wrote that theirs were noble and unselfish. In total, 115,000 Dutch Jews were deported to death camps, and only 5,450 returned.

Right: This photo shows the entrance to the annexe. Bep's father built a tightly fitting, hinged bookcase to hide it.

KALFF

13 July 1942

The van Pels family – Hermann, Auguste and Peter – join the Franks in the annexe.

6 August 1942

2,000 Jews are arrested in Amsterdam. They are sent to Westerbork deportation centre and on to Auschwitz.

During the day they could not use the toilet because pipes ran through the office. They had chamber pots under their beds. A tin tub served as a bath, but there was no privacy. Anne and Margot often bathed in the office on Saturdays when there was no one there. The curtains stayed closed, so they scrubbed in semi-darkness.

Food was basic. They kept some supplies in the annexe, and Miep and Bep shopped for fresh food, using false ration cards that Jan Gies had acquired. The local grocer guessed what was going on but never said anything. As war dragged on, fresh food became scarce. At one time, they lived on ersatz coffee (made from acorns) and a slice of bread for breakfast, with lettuce or spinach and potatoes for dinner. Anne and Margot were thin and very pale because they never went into the open air.

There were arguments, mostly about food: Anne thought Mr and Mrs van Pels ate too much. She was often irritated with the people around her.

Right: Otto Frank (seated, centre) surrounded by some of the helpers: Miep Gies (bottom left), Johannes Kleiman (top left), Victor Kugler (top right), and Bep Voskuijl (bottom right).

October–November 1942
British forces defeat the German army at El Alamein, North Africa.

16 November 1942
Fritz Pfeffer joins the Franks and van Pels in the annexe. Anne types up a list of rules for him.

Right: The annexe bathroom, shown here, had a sink and toilet. Anne complained that Mr van Pels dominated bathroom time.

Daily life

Anne typed out rules for daily life in the annexe, which she described as 'Temporary Accommodation for Jews'. Everyone had to speak softly at all times in a 'civilized' language, 'hence no German'. Mealtimes were 9 a.m. breakfast; 1:15–1:45 lunch; and dinner 'depending on news broadcasts'.

She thought being in hiding was hardest for her because she was the youngest. She complained that no one understood her. The van Pels said she was cheeky and had been badly brought up. Anne and Mr Pfeffer argued about Anne's using their room to study. Anne also quarrelled with her mother, which upset Edith. Otto acted as peacemaker.

At night there were constant air raids by British and American planes, trying to drive the Germans out of the Netherlands. Anne could not sleep through the raids and went into her father's room. She worried about being discovered and shot. There were narrow escapes. Burglars once broke into the office. They got as far as the bookcase that hid the annexe entrance and rattled it, while the terrified occupants waited anxiously. But the burglars went away.

The helpers did everything they could to assist their friends, calling in every day and bringing gifts and news from outside, where thousands of Dutch Jews were being sent to concentration camps.

December 1942
The annexe celebrates St Nicholas Day and the Jewish festival of Hanukkah.

March 1943
12,000 Jews a week are being deported from the Netherlands.

A Young Woman

Even in hiding, Anne loved fashion and wanted to look her best. She was growing into a young woman: she wrote about the changes to her body during puberty, and sometimes she thought about sex.

Anne spent hours looking at her face in the mirror. She bleached dark hairs above her lip and curled her hair into all sorts of styles. She grew taller and her clothes were far too small. She complained that her vest was halfway up her stomach. New clothes were impossible, but Miep managed to get her some new green shoes. Anne was shocked when she compared her old privileged life with life in the annexe.

Below: Anne shared this room with Mr Pfeffer. She put postcards and pictures of film stars on the wall to make the room homier. The window was papered over.

19 April–16 May 1943
Warsaw Uprising: Jewish resistance fighters rise up against the Nazis but the uprising is brutally suppressed.

25 July 1943
In Italy, Fascist leader Benito Mussolini is overthrown. The annexe celebrates the good news.

> '*We're Jews in chains, chained to one spot, without any rights....*
> *One day this terrible war will be over ... we'll be people again*
> *and not just Jews.*'
> Anne Frank, diary, 11 April 1944

Anne kept her sense of fun, joking and often acting the clown. She went through a dance and ballet phase, and made a modern dance costume from one of her mother's old petticoats, threading it with ribbon. Anne also became very thoughtful. She analyzed her relationship with her parents. She thought about God, religion and what it meant to her to be Jewish: she knew it was because they were Jewish that they were persecuted. Every Friday night, the annexe observed the start of the Sabbath, lighting candles and cooking whatever food was available.

Above: Mr Kugler brought Anne copies of this film magazine, *The Weekly*, so she could keep up to date with the latest news. He said it was the only Dutch magazine free of Nazi propaganda.

Otto tutored the three teenagers. Anne learned languages, history and shorthand. She loved history, Greek mythology and reading. She listened to the news on the radio and thought about politics. She read avidly, either her father's books, or books that Miep brought from the library. Sometimes, Anne felt isolated and she wanted someone to confide in. In 1944, she turned to Peter. They spent a lot of time together. For a while Anne thought she was in love. She confided in Margot and Otto, but after a few months, her feelings for Peter faded.

7 August 1943
Anne begins to write short stories as well as keeping her diary.

September 1943
Allied forces land in southern Italy. Hopes grow in the annexe for an end to the war.

The Holocaust

Between 1941 and 1945, the Nazis systematically murdered about 6 million European Jews. Starting in 1933, concentration camps were built to hold people considered 'undesirable', such as Communists. In 1941–42, death camps were built solely for the purpose of killing Jews. As German forces occupied different countries, they rounded up all the Jews. In the Soviet Union, about 1 million were shot. In Poland and elsewhere, Jews were forced into ghettos. After 1941, killing took place on a massive scale. Jews were loaded onto trains heading for death camps such as Auschwitz. There, thousands of men, women and children were led into chambers that looked like shower rooms, where they were killed by a cyanide compound known as Zyklon B, dropped into vents. Their bodies were burned, which gave the Holocaust (Greek for 'burnt whole') its name. Not all Jews and other prisoners were killed immediately: some were put to work as slave labourers.

This map shows the main death and concentration camps in Europe in 1944. The Nazis murdered 6 million Jews and 5 million non-Jews, including Communists, homosexuals, Romanies, disabled people, the elderly and Soviet prisoners of war.

JEWISH DEATHS

Two out of every three Jews in Europe died in the Holocaust. Some figures for the Jewish dead are
- Poland: 3 million
- Soviet Union: 1 million
- Hungary: 440,000
- Germany: 160,000
- The Netherlands: 109,000
- France: 83,000
- Other countries combined: 1.2 million

Left: Jewish prisoners in the camps were forced to sleep crammed together on tiered wooden boards. They wore rags and were given hardly any food. Thousands died of starvation and disease. When Allied forces liberated the camps in 1945, they found mounds of corpses, or skeletal survivors such as these Jewish men in Buchenwald.

Right: Nazis force eight-year-old Tsvi Nussbaum and other Jews out of the Warsaw Ghetto, May 1943. When Germany invaded Poland in 1939, 500,000 Jews lived in Warsaw. They were forced to live in a ghetto in appalling conditions. Many starved to death. In 1943, young Warsaw Jews fought back, but the armed uprising was crushed.

Below: A mountain of shoes at Auschwitz concentration camp gives some idea of the Holocaust's scale. Before going into the gas chambers, Jews were ordered to take off all their clothes. These shoes remain at Auschwitz today, as a reminder of those who were killed.

I Want to Be a Writer

By spring 1944, Anne had been in hiding for nearly two years. The course of the war had changed in favour of the Allies. There were rumours that the Allies would invade soon and that war would end. Anne began to be optimistic.

Anne had decided she wanted to be a writer someday. She spent hours writing in her diary, sitting in her parents' room or at a desk in the attic. She covered every detail of life in the annexe and confided her most intimate thoughts to her diary. When she finished the diary her father had given her, the helpers gave her office books or sheets of office paper to write on. Everyone knew about Anne's diary and how important it was to her.

In 1943, Anne began writing short stories. Some were based on real-life events in the annexe. Others were fictional, often highly imaginative fairy tales. They were later published as *Tales from the Secret Annexe*.

In March 1944, Anne heard a Dutch programme on the radio. It was broadcast from London. The minister for education called on Dutch people to keep their personal documents, such as letters and diaries. When the war was over, they would be stored in a special centre so there would be a record of how ordinary people had been forced to live during the war.

> '*My greatest wish is to be a journalist and later on a famous writer.*'
> Anne Frank, diary, 11 May 1944

14 October 1943

Jews in Sobibor death camp rise up. 600 Jews break out. Some join partisan units but few survive the war.

December 1943

Anne has influenza. She takes all sorts of remedies and sucks cough drops to try to stop herself from coughing.

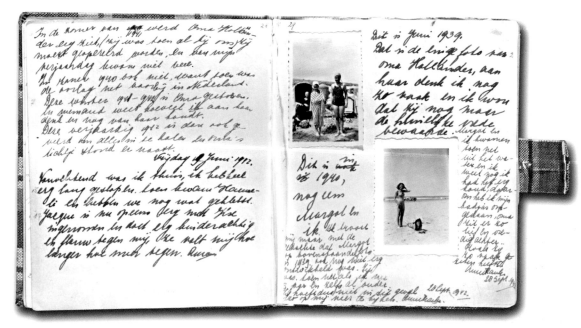

Above: These are actual pages from Anne's diary. She pasted in the photograph of Margot and her on the beach, when she was 11.

Dearest Kitty

Anne wrote her diary in the form of letters to an imaginary person called Kitty. All the entries began 'Dearest Kitty'. Anne probably took the name from a character in one of her favourite books, *Joop ter Heul* by Cissy van Marx, which was very popular with young Dutch girls at the time.

Everyone in the annexe immediately thought of Anne's diaries.

Anne began revising her diary with the idea of having it published after the war. In May, she also started to write it as a book, which she intended to call *Het Achterhuis* (*The House Behind*). She wrote the new version on sheets of coloured paper. On her 15th birthday, in June 1944, Miep and Bep gave her a few blank ledger books as a birthday present so that she could carry on with her writing.

December 1943

The annexe celebrates Christmas. Miep bakes a cake with 'Peace 1944' written on top of it.

March 1944

Anne hears a Dutch radio broadcast asking for people to keep their letters and diaries as a wartime record.

DISCOVERY AND
DEPORTATION

4

Discovered

Anne wrote her last diary entry on 1 August 1944. She was 15. Three days later, the German secret police, the Gestapo, arrived.

The morning of 4 August had begun as usual. Miep, Bep, Kleiman and Kugler were in the office, while the residents of the secret annexe went about their normal tasks. At about 10:30 a.m., a car arrived at 263 Prinsengracht and a number of men got out. One was a Gestapo officer, Karl Silberbauer; the others were Dutch Nazis. They walked into the office, pointed a gun at Victor Kugler, and demanded to see the Jews in hiding. They were taken upstairs to the annexe, where Edith was standing by a table. Kugler announced that the Gestapo had arrived. Anne and the other occupants were rounded up and stood in the sitting room, their hands above their heads. Margot wept, while Anne stood completely silent.

Silberbauer told the occupants to pack. He told them to bring out their valuables and picked up a briefcase to pack them in. It held Anne's writings – notebooks, diaries and loose sheets of paper. They fell onto the floor.

'A bundle of contradictions'

In her last diary entry, Anne said she had two parts to her personality: one was a flippant, boy-chasing flirt, the other a deeper, purer and finer person that very few people ever saw.

Previous page: Railway tracks lead to the entrance of Auschwitz-Birkenau death camp. Some 1.1 million Jews died here; it was known as the 'death factory'.

6 June 1944
D-Day: Allied forces land in France. The Allied invasion of occupied Europe has begun.

Mid-July 1944
The Soviet army enters Poland. They liberate Majdanek death camp and take photographs of the horrors they find.

Anne said nothing and did not pick them up. While Anne and the others packed, Silberbauer spoke to Otto, asking how long they had been in hiding. He did not believe they had remained hidden for two years. To show Silberbauer evidence of the time they had spent in the annexe, Otto pointed to marks on the wall, where he had measured Anne's height over the years.

Everyone filed down to the front office. Miep noticed how very pale Anne was – she had not been in the air for two years. The Franks, the van Pels and Fritz Pfeffer were taken to a gaol in the centre of town. They were pushed into a room filled with bunk beds and only buckets to use as toilets.

Betrayal or carelessness?

No one knows who betrayed the Franks. There were two official inquiries after the war, and a few suspects. But nothing was proved. Perhaps people in the annexe were becoming careless. Probably no one will ever know.

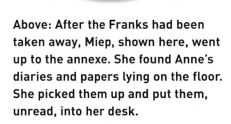

Above: After the Franks had been taken away, Miep, shown here, went up to the annexe. She found Anne's diaries and papers lying on the floor. She picked them up and put them, unread, into her desk.

25 July 1944
Operation Cobra: US forces fight their way off the Normandy beaches and move forward into central France.

4 August 1944
Anne and her companions from the secret annexe are discovered and arrested.

Westerbork

Four days after their arrest, Anne and the others, together with other Jewish prisoners, were put on a train to Westerbork, a transit camp in the northeast Netherlands. During the journey, Anne gazed out of the window at the passing countryside.

Westerbork was a strange place. Surrounded by barbed-wire fences and tall watchtowers, it was like a small town. There were more than 100 barracks for people to sleep in, as well as workshops, a hospital, a school and a restaurant.

Below: At any one time, 30,000 Jews were kept in Westerbork, waiting to be sent east.

Summer 1944

As Germany begins to lose the war, they destroy camps and force Jews on so-called death marches to Germany.

8 August 1944

Anne arrives in Westerbork.

Daily life was reasonably comfortable, but this gave a false sense of security: every Tuesday, Jews were chosen to be sent to Auschwitz.

On arrival at Westerbork, Anne and her companions were searched. Because they had been in hiding, they were labelled 'convict' Jews and put into a punishment barracks, with little freedom. They were given blue overalls and wooden clogs. Anne's hair was cut. The next morning they were put to work, taking apart old aeroplane batteries. It was filthy work, and dust from the batteries made Anne cough. Every day was the same: roll-call at five in the morning, work, then lunch, which consisted of a piece of dry bread and some watery soup, and work again. The Franks became well known and were very much liked. Anne and Margot made friends with two Dutch sisters – Lientje and Janny – who worked at the next bench.

About a month after their arrival, a guard entered the barracks with a list of those who were to be deported to Auschwitz. More than 1,000 names were called, including the Franks, the van Pels and Mr Pfeffer. The next day, they were loaded onto a train bound for Auschwitz.

A dreadful journey

The journey to Auschwitz took three days. The train consisted of freight wagons. More than 70 Jews were pushed into each wagon, without food, light or heat. There were two buckets in each wagon, one filled with water, the other for a toilet. The stench was appalling. There was hardly room to sit. One survivor remembered Anne trying to look out of the window, sleeping or talking quietly with Margot and Peter.

31 August 1944
The Soviet army enters Bucharest, capital of Romania, and moves on to Bulgaria.

3 September 1944
Anne leaves Westerbork on the last transport ever to depart Westerbork for Auschwitz concentration camp.

Auschwitz

When the train arrived at Auschwitz, men in striped clothing – leaders of the prisoner work gangs, known as 'kapos', banged on the sides, pulling people out and shouting. SS officers with ferocious dogs marched up and down the platform, carrying whips. Anne got out of the train into glaring searchlights.

When Jews arrived at Auschwitz, they were lined up on the platform for 'selection', choosing who would go straight to the gas chamber and who would be admitted to the camp. Those sent to the left – usually the sick, elderly and young children – died. Those on the right lived. Anne and six of her companions were sent to the right. Mr van Pels was sent to the gas chamber in early October 1944.

Below: Babies and very young children were killed as soon as they arrived in Auschwitz. Some older children were used for work or experiments. This photo was taken when the Soviets liberated the camp on 27 January 1945. Only 180 children were still alive.

6 September 1944

Anne arrives at Auschwitz and is sent to Auschwitz-Birkenau with her sister and mother.

Early October 1944

Mr van Pels is sent to the gas chamber.

'The Frank girls kept very much to themselves.... They looked terrible. Their hands and bodies were covered with spots and sores.'

Ronnie Goldstein-van Cleef, survivor

Women and men were ordered to form separate groups. People cried as families were divided. Anne's father, Mr Pfeffer and Peter, together with other men, were marched off. Otto never saw his family again. Anne and the other women were marched into the women's section of Auschwitz-Birkenau. Their heads were shaved and they were given shoes and a sacklike dress to wear. Their arms were tattooed with a number and they were taken to their hut, which was filthy and freezing, with wooden bunks. There was no soap and hardly any food. The toilet was a long bench with holes over a pit.

Every day, the women were woken at 3:30 a.m. They stood for nearly an hour while they were counted. They worked all day, digging up grass in a field. Anne and Margot's health got worse. They had scabies, an itchy rash caused by parasitic mites.

Death factory

There were three camps at Auschwitz. Auschwitz I was a concentration camp for Polish political prisoners. Auschwitz II, or Auschwitz-Birkenau, was a death camp for Jews and Romanies. It contained four crematoria. The third camp, Auschwitz-Monowitz, was a slave-labour camp.

On 28 October, a selection took place. Women were marched into a hall in front of an SS doctor, perhaps Josef Mengele, who was notorious for cruel experiments on Jewish children. He decided Anne and Margot should be sent to another camp. Left behind, Edith died on 6 January 1945.

23 October 1944
Allied forces liberate Paris from Nazi occupation.

28 October 1944
Anne and Margot are sent to Bergen-Belsen concentration camp in Germany.

Bergen-Belsen

Anne and Margot, together with some 600 other women, were sent to Bergen-Belsen, a concentration camp in Germany. They were given old clothes and shoes, a blanket, some bread, sausage and a piece of margarine. The journey to Bergen-Belsen took five days. The train was freezing and cramped, and they were given no more food.

When Anne and Margot reached Bergen-Belsen, they were put in a tent with other women. The women slept on the floor. Their toilet was an open pit outside. After a while, Anne, Margot and others were moved to a freezing stone hut, filled with tiered wooden platforms, or bunks.

Lientje and Janny Brilleslijper, the Dutch sisters from Westerbork, were in the bunk above Anne and Margot. They formed a little group, trying to support each other. They had only one blanket each to keep warm. At night, Anne told jokes and stories, trying to keep their spirits up.

Conditions in Bergen-Belsen were unspeakable. Thousands of Jews were being sent there from camps in the east. All basic services – food, water and sanitation – had collapsed. Many prisoners had typhus, a deadly infectious disease spread by lice, which causes fever, delirium and violent diarrhoea.

'The two [Anne and Margot] were inseparable like my sister and I. They looked like two frozen birds, it was painful to look at them.'

Lientje Brilleslijper, remembering Anne and Margot Frank

6 January 1945
Edith Frank dies in Auschwitz-Birkenau.

27 January 1945
Soviet soldiers liberate Auschwitz: Otto Frank and the other surviving Jews are freed.

Right: There were no gas chambers at Bergen-Belsen. Instead, prisoners slowly starved to death or died from disease and brutality. This 12-year-old girl was photographed after the camp was liberated.

There were no showers, soap, medicines or toilets. Prisoners used latrine pits, if they were strong enough to walk or crawl from their bunk. As people died, their bodies piled up.

Anne and her friends were put to work, taking apart old shoes by hand. It was pointless, difficult and painful work. Anne and Lientje's hands bled and they became infected. To help their group, Anne and Lientje tried to beg or steal food from the camp kitchen. They were often punished. In November, Mrs van Pels arrived in Bergen-Belsen. She found Anne and Margot and joined their small group.

Hanukkah

Even in the misery of Bergen-Belsen, Anne and her friends tried to celebrate Hanukkah. They saved scraps of bread, Anne found a piece of garlic and Lientje had some cabbage. They sat together singing Jewish songs.

February 1945
Lies Goslar, Anne's school friend from Amsterdam, arrives in Bergen-Belsen.

February 1945
British and US planes bomb Dresden in Germany, killing 10,000 civilians.

Death

In February 1945, Anne's friend Lies arrived in Bergen-Belsen. She met Mrs van Pels, who gave Anne the news. The two girls were in different parts of the camp. They met on either side of a barbed-wire fence and cried.

Anne told her friend that they had been in hiding for two years, and not in Switzerland at all. Anne also told Lies they had nothing to eat in their part of the camp. Lies's barracks were receiving some food from the Red Cross. That night, Lies came to the fence with a small bundle containing a jacket, some biscuits, sugar and a tin

Above: British troops liberated Bergen-Belsen on 15 April 1945. They found 60,000 starving prisoners, including these Jewish women. There were 10,000 dead bodies in the camp.

of sardines. She threw the parcel over the fence but heard a dreadful cry from Anne. Another woman had seized the parcel. The next night, Lies brought another parcel, which Anne caught. It was the last time Lies saw her friend.

> 'I want to be useful or bring enjoyment to all people, even those I've never met. I want to go on living, even after my death!'
>
> Anne Frank, diary, 5 April 1944

March 1945

Margot and Anne Frank die within days of each other. They are buried in a mass grave.

30 April 1945

Adolf Hitler commits suicide as Germany faces defeat.

By now, Margot was ill with dysentery, a severe form of diarrhoea. She was weak and exhausted. The two sisters were sent to a barrack full of sick and dying people. There was no water or food. Lientje and Janny brought them whatever they could find. A typhus epidemic was raging through the camp. Anne and Margot became feverish and gravely ill with typhus. The hut was freezing, and Anne constantly pleaded for the door to be closed. Margot fell from her bunk onto the stone floor and died. Anne was covered with lice, so she threw away her clothes and wore only a thin blanket. She died a few days after her sister, some time during March. She was 15 years old.

Fate of the annexe

Otto Frank was the only one of the eight people from the annexe to survive the Holocaust.

- Hermann van Pels died in Auschwitz in early October 1944
- Fritz Pfeffer died in Neuengamme concentration camp, Germany, on 20 December 1944
- Edith Frank died in Auschwitz on 6 January 1945
- Margot Frank died in Bergen-Belsen in March 1945
- Anne Frank died in Bergen-Belsen in March 1945
- Auguste van Pels died somewhere in Germany or Czechoslovakia probably between 9 April and 8 May 1945
- Peter van Pels died in Mauthausen concentration camp, Austria, on 5 May 1945

Right: Lientje and Janny found Anne's and Margot's bodies behind the sick barracks and laid them in a mass grave. In 1999, this memorial stone was erected at Bergen-Belsen.

MARGOT FRANK 1926 – 1945
ANNE FRANK 1929 – 1945
נר ה׳ נשמת אדם
(SPRÜCHE 20 27)

7 May 1945

Germany surrenders to the Allies. In August, Japan surrenders and World War II ends.

3 June 1945

Otto Frank returns to Amsterdam and is soon reunited with Lies Goslar and Miep and Jan Gies.

Story of a Diary

Anne's father returned to Amsterdam in June 1945. Miep, Jan, Mr Kugler and Mr Kleiman were already there. Otto knew Edith had died, but he hoped Anne and Margot were still alive. In July, he heard from Lientje and Janny that they had died. Lies Goslar told him of her meeting with Anne. Miep had kept Anne's diaries and writings: now she gave them to Otto, telling him they were Anne's legacy to him.

The diaries brought back painful memories, but Otto decided they should be published. At first he took out some of the more personal details but later reinstated them. The first version was published in 1947; since then the diary has been republished many times.

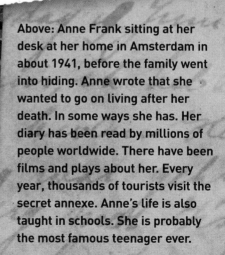

Above: Anne Frank sitting at her desk at her home in Amsterdam in about 1941, before the family went into hiding. Anne wrote that she wanted to go on living after her death. In some ways she has. Her diary has been read by millions of people worldwide. There have been films and plays about her. Every year, thousands of tourists visit the secret annexe. Anne's life is also taught in schools. She is probably the most famous teenager ever.

Left: Otto Frank stands in what was the secret annexe. In 1960, the building officially opened as the Anne Frank House. It contains the Opekta offices and the annexe. Otto died in 1980.

20th Century-Fox is Honoured to Present

GEORGE STEVENS'

production of

THE **DIARY** OF

ANNE

FRANK

MILLIE PERKINS AS ANNE FRANK · JOSEPH SCHILDKRAUT · SHELLEY WINTERS

RICHARD BEYMER · GUSTI HUBER and ED WYNN

PRODUCED AND DIRECTED BY GEORGE STEVENS · SCREENPLAY BY FROM THE PLAY BY FRANCES GOODRICH AND ALBERT HACKETT

A 20th CENTURY-FOX

CINEMASCOPE PICTURE

Above: This film version of Anne Frank's diary premiered in 1959. It starred actress Shelley Winters as Mrs van Pels and Millie Perkins as Anne Frank. It won three Oscars. The Dutch royal family were present at the premiere.

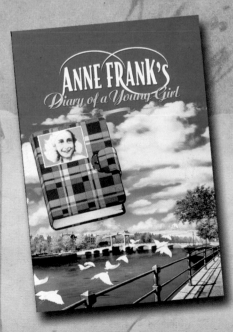

THE PUBLISHED DIARY

The first edition of Anne Frank's diary was published in Dutch, in 1947. It sold out almost immediately. A second and third printing followed within a year. In 1950, German and French editions appeared, and two years later it was published in Britain and the United States. It has been translated into more than 70 languages and has sold more than 30 million copies. Anne was one of 1.5 million children who died in the Holocaust; she remains the most famous.

Glossary

Allies twenty-six nations that fought against Nazi Germany and the other Axis powers, including Japan and Italy. Leading Allied nations included Britain, the United States and the Soviet Union.

annexe addition; an extra building; to annexe something is to add it on or to absorb it.

anti-Semitism hatred and persecution of Jewish people. The word 'Semitic' describes a group of languages that include Hebrew; it is often used to describe Jews.

Auschwitz a massive complex that was the largest of all the Nazi death camps. Approximately 1.1 million Jews were killed in Auschwitz, which is in modern Poland.

Axis powers Germany, Italy, Japan and other countries that were allied with Nazi Germany during World War II.

Bergen-Belsen concentration camp in northern Germany. This was the camp where Anne and Margot Frank died.

boycott to refuse to buy, sell or use.

Communist someone who believes in Communism or is a member of the Communist Party. Communists aim to create an equal society in which all industry and agriculture are owned and run by the people.

concentration camps prison camps where Jews and others, such as Romanies and Communists, were held captive and worked to death.

crematoria furnaces for burning dead bodies.

death camps also called extermination camps; these were places where Jews and others were deliberately and systematically murdered, usually by poison gas.

demilitarized zone an area where military activity is not allowed.

deportation forced removal of Jews in Nazi-occupied countries from their homes to concentration, labour and death camps.

ersatz substitute; a poor-quality replacement.

Fascist supporter of Benito Mussolini's Fascist Party, an extreme nationalist political party that emerged in Italy in the 1920s and governed the country until 1943.

genocide acts committed with the intention of destroying, in whole or in part, an ethnic, racial or religious group. Such acts include murder, causing physical or mental harm, inflicting conditions of life calculated to bring about the group's destruction, imposing measures intended to prevent childbirth, and forcibly removing children from the group.

ghetto walled-off area in a town or city where Jews were forced to live.

Hanukkah the eight-day Jewish festival of lights, celebrated around the same time as the Christian festival of Christmas.

Hebrew the language of the Jewish holy books. The official language of modern Israel.

Holocaust the deliberate and systematic persecution and murder of more than 6 million Jews by Nazi Germany. The term comes from the Greek words 'holo' (whole) and 'kaustos' (burn), meaning 'a sacrifice that is completely consumed by fire'.

kosher food that is prepared in such a way that it is acceptable under Jewish law.

labour camps places where Jews and prisoners of war were used as slave labour to produce goods for the German war effort. Most people were worked to death.

Liberal Jews members of the Jewish religion who do not follow the Jewish laws in a strict way.

liberation the freeing of prisoners from the concentration camps by Allied forces.

Nazi member of the National Socialist German Workers' Party, or Nazi Party, the extreme political party led by Adolf Hitler that governed Germany from 1933 to 1945.

partisan unit a small group of civilians fighting against enemy troops using guerrilla tactics such as surprise raids.

Passover (Pesach) Jewish religious festival that commemorates the time when God 'passed over' the Israelites in order to punish the Egyptians who were holding them captive as slaves.

pogrom systematic violence against Jews, often with the support of the government.

propaganda information that is put out by governments and other organizations to influence what people think and do.

ration card an official card that permits the bearer an allowance of food when it is in short supply, as during wartime.

refugee someone who flees persecution or danger in their country and seeks safety in another part of the world.

rheumatic fever a serious disease with symptoms including fever, swollen joints and inflammation, or swelling, of the heart.

Romanies a people (often incorrectly known as Gypsies), probably of Indian origin, who live scattered through Europe and the Americas and maintain a nomadic lifestyle. Between 200,000 and 800,000 Romanies died in the Holocaust.

Sabbath (Shabbat) the Jewish day of rest and prayer, which runs from before sundown on Friday to after nightfall on Saturday.

seder a special meal eaten during Passover (Pesach). The foods are symbolic. They include lettuce, signifying the food eaten during slavery; horseradish for the misery of slavery; egg for new life; and herbs for spring.

Soviet Union the USSR (Union of Soviet Socialist Republics). It included Russia and was the world's first Communist state. It lasted from 1922 to 1991 and, today, has split into many separate countries, including Russia, Ukraine, Latvia, Estonia, Lithuania and Kazakhstan.

Star of David six-pointed Jewish symbol that the Nazis forced Jews to wear. It was usually yellow.

swastika an ancient religious symbol that was adopted by the Nazi Party, now banned in Germany.

Westerbork transit camp in the northeastern Netherlands, where Jews, including the Franks, and others were kept before being sent on to death camps such as Auschwitz.

Yiddish mixture of Hebrew and German that originated among the Jews of Eastern Europe.

Bibliography

The Diary of a Young Girl: Definitive Edition, Frank, Anne, ed. Otto Frank and Mirjam Pressler, published by Penguin Books, 2001

Tales from the Secret Annexe (stories, essays, fables and reminiscences written in hiding), Frank, Anne, published by Penguin Books, 1986

Anne Frank, Poole, Josephine, and Barrett, Angela, published by Hutchinson, 2005

Anne Frank's Story, Lee, Carol Ann, published by Puffin Books, 2001

Holocaust, Adams, Simon, published by Franklin Watts, 2005

Roses from the Earth: The Biography of Anne Frank, Lee, Carol Ann, published by Penguin Books, 2000

Sources of quotes:

p. 8 *The Diary of a Young Girl*, Penguin, 2001, p. 28

p. 21 *The Diary of a Young Girl*, Penguin, 2001, p. 7

p. 22 *Roses from the Earth*, Carol Ann Lee, Penguin, 2000, p. 31

p. 22 'Do You Remember? Reminiscences of My School Days', *Tales from the Secret Annexe*, Penguin, 1986, p. 93

p. 29 *Roses from the Earth*, Carol Ann Lee, Penguin, 2000, p. 34

p. 31 *The Diary of a Young Girl*, Penguin, 2001, p. 8

p. 34 *The Diary of a Young Girl*, Penguin, 2001, p. 1

p. 36 *The Diary of a Young Girl*, Penguin, 2001, p. 144

p. 39 *The Diary of a Young Girl*, Penguin, 2001, p. 68

p. 41 *The Diary of a Young Girl*, Penguin, 2001, p. 261

p. 44 *The Diary of a Young Girl*, Penguin, 2001, p. 294

p. 53 *Roses from the Earth*, Carol Ann Lee, Penguin, 2000, p. 176

p. 54 *Roses from the Earth*, Carol Ann Lee, Penguin, 2000, p. 181

p. 56 *The Diary of a Young Girl*, Penguin, 2001, p. 250

Some Web sites that will help you find out more about Anne Frank and the Holocaust:

www.annefrank.ch
Web site of the Anne Frank–Fonds, Basel, Switzerland, of which Anne's cousin Buddy Elias is the president.

www.annefrank.org
The Web site of the Anne Frank House in Amsterdam.

www.annefrank.com
The Anne Frank Center USA, with online exhibitions.

www.ushmm.org/wlc/en/
A Holocaust encyclopedia run by the United States Holocaust Memorial Museum.

www.teacheroz.com/holocaust.htm
Extensive information and links about the Holocaust.

fcit.usf.edu/Holocaust/people/children.htm
A Web site devoted to children's experiences of the Holocaust.

Index

Acknowledgments

Sources: Getty/AFFB = Getty/Anne Frank–Fonds, Basel/Anne Frank House, Amsterdam

B = bottom, C = centre, T = top

Front cover: Getty/AFFB.

1 Getty/AFFB; **3** Getty/AFFB; **7** Getty/AFFB; **8** Getty/AFFB; **9** Getty/AFFB; **10B** AKG Images/Abraham Pisarek; **10C** Corbis/Richard T Nowitz; **11** AKG Images/Abraham Pisarek; **13** Getty/AFFB; **14–15** Getty/AFFB; **16** AKG Images; **17** Scala, Florence/HIP; **19** Getty/AFFB; **20–21** Getty/AFFB; **23** Getty/AFFB; **24** Getty/AFFB; **25** United States Holocaust Memorial Museum; **26** AKG Images; **27** Getty/Hulton Archive; **28** Getty/AFFB; **29** Ronald Grant Archives; **30** Getty/Hulton Archive; **33–38** Getty/AFFB; **39** AKG Images/Michael Teller; **40** Getty/AFFB; **41** Ronald Grant Archives; **42–43B** AKG Images; **43T** Art Archive/National Archives, Washington; **43C** AKG Images; **45** Getty/AFFB; **47** Corbis/Carmen Redondo; **49** Getty/AFFB; **50** Herinneringscentrum Kamp Westerbork/Nederlands Instituut voor Oorlogsdocumentatie; **52** AKG Images; **55** United States Holocaust Memorial Museum/Maurice Raynor; **56** The Research House; **57** Alamy/David Crausby; **58T** Getty/AFFB; **58B** Getty Images; **59** Ronald Grant Archives.

The publishers would particularly like to thank Buddy Elias, Christoph Knoch, and all at the Anne Frank–Fonds, Basel and the Anne Frank House, Amsterdam.